מסורה

ArtScroll Youth Series®

A Dov Dov Book

DOV DOV AND THE
TREASURE BOX
and other stories

by Yona Weinberg

illustrated by Liat Benyaminy Ariel

FIRST EDITION
First Impression . . . November, 1991

Published and Distributed by
MESORAH PUBLICATIONS, Ltd.
Brooklyn, New York 11232

Distributed in Israel by
MESORAH MAFITZIM / J. GROSSMAN
Rechov Harav Uziel 117
Jerusalem, Israel

Distributed in Australia & New Zealand by
GOLD'S BOOK & GIFT CO.
36 William Street
Balaclava 3183, Vic., Australia

Distributed in Europe by
J. LEHMANN HEBREW BOOKSELLERS
20 Cambridge Terrace
Gateshead, Tyne and Wear
England NE8 1RP

Distributed in South Africa by
KOLLEL BOOKSHOP
22 Muller Street
Yeoville 2198
Johannesburg, South Africa

ARTSCROLL YOUTH SERIES ®
DOV DOV AND THE TREASURE BOX AND OTHER STORIES
© *Copyright 1991, by* YONA WEINBERG *and* MESORAH PUBLICATIONS, Ltd.
4401 Second Avenue / Brooklyn, N.Y. 11232 / (718) 921-9000

Typography by CompuScribe at ArtScroll Studios, Ltd.
4401 Second Avenue / Brooklyn, N.Y. 11232 / (718) 921-9000

Printed in the United States of America by
EDISON LITHOGRAPHING AND PRINTING CORP.
Bound by Sefercraft, Quality Bookbinders, Ltd. Brooklyn, N.Y.

Table of Contents

Dov Dov and the Treasure Box

ov Dov locked his door and pulled the shades down. He went to take out his secret box from under his bed.

"Are you ready, Dov?" asked Aryeh, waiting on the other side of the door.

"Not yet," answered Dov Dov. He groped under the bed to reach for his treasure box. It was a red metal box that looked like a chocolate gift box, but inside Dov Dov kept all his prize collection.

A beautiful blue and green crystal-clear marble he won at a game; a locust shell he found the summer before, a leftover from the seventeen-year locusts; a picture postcard of a volcano erupting that his uncle had sent him from Seattle; a negative of his cavity-filled tooth; a few golden-orange and red leaves that were so unusual and beautiful they sometimes took his breath away; a plastic key chain that said "Keep Smiling;" some sea shells with unusual shapes; a broken watch his mother had given him; a snake's skin he had found in the woods behind his school; a mini-globe; a compass; a police whistle; a Nebraska mini-license plate; and a small plastic plunger he found in the garage.

This was Dov Dov's collection and it meant more to him than all his toys. It was his and his alone. Whenever he was in the mood, he took out his box and enjoyed his treasure.

Now he needed to add to his collection. Aryeh had just given him a small pebble, so smooth and white it shown like a jewel.

"Dov Dov, are you ready?" called Aryeh again, from behind the door.

"Not yet." Where was his box? Dov Dov reached further under the bed. The box was gone! But how could that be? No one was in his room alone the whole morning. No one except for Aryeh. But Aryeh wouldn't have taken his treasure box. Would he? The question rose in Dov Dov's mind like waves under a stormy wind.

Dov Dov opened the door. "It's gone," he said. He stared straight into Aryeh's face.

"Gone? How could it be gone?"

"I don't know but it's not where I always keep it."

"Maybe you put it somewhere else and you just forgot," said Aryeh.

"I don't think so," Dov Dov said. He went to ask his mother.

"I haven't seen your box, Dov Dov, but I'm sure it will turn up." She smiled at Dov Dov. When she smiled, her eyes crinkled up in the corners and her face lit up.

"By the way, Dov Dov, I'm making your favorite supper for your birthday today."

"Oh boy! Thanks, Mom!"

"Today's your birthday?" Aryeh asked.

"Yes," Dov Dov smiled happily. "And my mom always makes my favorite supper for my birthday, homemade pizza with her special sauce that takes a long time to make, and watermelon for dessert."

"Mmm . . . it sounds delicious."

"Mom, can Aryeh stay over for supper?"

"Sure, I don't see why not. Just ask your mom, Aryeh, if it's okay with her."

Aryeh went to call home. Dov Dov followed him. Could Aryeh

have taken his box? I guess he could have, thought Dov Dov, but he would be *dan lechaf zechus*, he would judge him favorably. Maybe Aryeh was right. Maybe he had left it somewhere else.

"My mother said I could stay," said Aryeh.

"Great!"

"You sure are lucky, Dov Dov. Your parents are so nice."

"Dov Dov!" called Faigy, Dov Dov's younger sister, her fluffy curls bouncing softly on her shoulders, and her eyes wide and innocent. "There was no candy."

"No candy where?" asked Dov Dov. He didn't know what Faigy was talking about.

"The candy from your candy box. I looked inside but there was no candy."

"Faigy!" Dov Dov yelled. "Did you take my treasure box?"

Faigy shrank back. "I'm sorry," she whispered, her lower lip sticking out. "It was on your bed. I thought it was a candy box. It looked like the candy box we got last Purim for *shalach manos.*"

"It is the same box we got for *shalach manos* last Purim," Dov Dov explained. "Mrs. Englander sent it to us but after the chocolates were finished, Abba gave the box to me to keep. Now I use it to hold my private collection in it."

"I'm sorry. I didn't know."

"That's okay, but where is the box now?" Dov Dov followed Faigy to her room. She took down her doll from her shelf and underneath was the treasure box.

"Here! I'm sorry. I won't take it again without asking first."

"Okay!" Dov Dov smiled and looked at Aryeh. He was glad he had been *dan lechaf zechus.*

"Dov Dov," called his mother, "Abba will be home soon. Why don't you go outside and play until he comes?"

"Okay, Mom." Dov Dov took his ball and went out.

The day was like a spring day, warm with promises. The sky was clear with little fluffy clouds drifting aimlessly across it, and the sun was rising along the arc of the sky.

Dov Dov and Aryeh played catch in the backyard. "What are you getting for your birthday?" asked Aryeh, as he threw the ball.

Dov Dov caught it. "I don't know, but I know it's going to be a surprise. A big surprise."

"How do you know, and what kind of a surprise?"

Dov Dov laughed and ran after the ball. "I can't tell you but I know it is going to be a surprise. It's a different kind of surprise."

"I love surprises," said Aryeh. He jumped up to catch the ball and landed in a puddle. "Oh, no!" Aryeh laughed. Dov Dov laughed too. "Let's go inside and clean up."

Just then Dov Dov's father drove up. "Hi, Abba!"

"Hi, Dov Dov! Happy birthday, King!" His father had a slow, gentle way of speaking.

Dov Dov laughed. He ran to help his father carry his bags. "What's in the bag, Abba?"

"An ice cream cake I picked up for you on the way home."

"Oh, boy! Thanks, Abba."

"Dov Dov!" called his mother. "Time to wash up for supper." She looked at the boys and shook her head. "How can two boys get so dirty just waiting in the yard?"

Dov Dov and Aryeh scooted upstairs to wash up. Faigy was the first one sitting at the table.

"Your pizza smells great, Mrs. Cohen, I am an expert on good food," said Aryeh. Dov Dov's father handed him a slice. The hot cheese was spread thickly over the thin dough and the sauce bubbled and sizzled.

"You will now experience a little *olam hazeh* as you taste this scrumptious, mouth-watering taste of Mrs. Cohen's homemade birthday pizza."

Dov Dov laughed. His father loved making kidding remarks to cheer everyone up.

Dov Dov took a small bite of his hot pizza. He looked at his father and mother. How lucky he was to have such parents. His father grinned at him, his eyes twinkling. The kitchen encircled him in a shell of warm security. He felt safe and cozy like a rabbit snug in its hole. He had parents who loved him and understood him so well.

"Oh, here, Dov Dov," said his father, removing something from his pocket. "I brought you this for your collection."

"What is it, Abba?" His father was often bringing him unusual articles for his treasure box.

"It's a stamp from Australia. I got a letter today from Menachem and Rita, and I saved the stamp for you."

"Does it have a picture of a kangaroo on it?" Dov Dov asked.

"No, it's a platypus."

"A platypus? Is that a kind of kitten?" asked Faigy.

"No," said Dov Dov's father. "A platypus is a small animal that lives in Australia. It has webbed feet and a fleshy bill like a duck's. Here, Dov Dov."

"Thanks, Abba!" Dov Dov left the table and ran up the stairs two at a time.

"Why don't you put it away after the meal, Dov Dov?" asked his mother. Dov Dov's answer was muffled from the steps.

"He sure is taking a long time," said Aryeh. He was just about to follow Dov Dov when Dov Dov returned, his face beaming. He was holding a package wrapped in plain white paper and tied with a red string.

"Is this the surprise?" asked Aryeh.

"Yes!" Dov Dov handed the package to his mother and father.

"Hey, what's going on?" Aryeh asked. "Isn't it your birthday, Dov Dov? How come you're giving your parents a present on your birthday?"

Dov Dov didn't answer. He looked at his parents. His parents looked back at him, a quizzical expression on their faces.

"Abba . . . Mommy . . . You're always doing things for me and giving me things. Today, on my birthday, I want to give *you* a gift."

Everyone was quiet as Dov Dov handed his homemade card to his parents.

DEAR ABBA AND MOMMY,

YOU GIVE ME FOOD AND CLOTHING, TAKE CARE OF ME WHEN I'M SICK, DRIVE ME TO SCHOOL. NOTHING IS TOO HARD FOR YOU TO DO IF YOU KNOW IT'S GOING TO BE GOOD FOR ME. YOU CHEER ME UP WHEN I'M SAD, YOU LISTEN TO MY PROBLEMS AND HELP ME FIGURE OUT WHAT TO DO. YOU'RE ALWAYS THERE WHEN I NEED YOU AND YOU NEVER COMPLAIN WHEN I NUDGE YOU. I LOVE YOU BECAUSE OF EVERYTHING YOU DO FOR ME AND BECAUSE YOU'RE MY ABBA AND MOMMY. HAPPY BIRTH-DAY TO ME!

TODAY ON MY BIRTHDAY I WANT TO GIVE YOU A SPECIAL PRESENT, TO THANK YOU AND SHOW YOU HOW MUCH I LOVE YOU. I HOPE YOU ENJOY MY PRESENT AS MUCH AS I DO.

Dov Dov's father looked at Dov Dov and blew his nose. His mother's eyes were glistening.

"Open it," Dov Dov prompted them. Dov Dov's mother carefully unwrapped the precious gift. Slowly . . . slowly . . . the wrapping paper peeled off. Dov Dov's parents stared at the present, their mouths slightly open. They looked at Dov Dov in disbelief.

"Your treasure box!"

Dov Dov smiled happily. "It's for you. It's the nicest present I could think of giving you."

Dov Dov's mother hugged him tightly.

"And don't worry about me," said Dov Dov. "I'm going to start a new treasure box right away. I found something upstairs for my first collection."

"What is it, Dov Dov?" asked Faigy. Dov Dov reached into his pocket and pulled out a small gray cottony ball.

"A spider's nest!"

What's Mine Is Yours;
What's Yours Is Mine

inney sneaked into the store and turned around to make sure he wasn't being followed. He crept in quietly and closed the door behind him.

Whew! So far, so good! Ari hadn't seen him.

"What can I do for you, Pinney?" asked Reb Yankel, the owner of the *sefarim* store.

"Hi, Reb Yankel. I'm here to buy my brother a present."

"All right," said Reb Yankel, walking towards the back of the store. "Any special occasion?"

"Well, you see," said Pinney, *"yom tov* is coming up and I happen to know Ari is anxious to buy that new *sefer* on the *gedolim* that just came out. I thought I would surprise him and buy it for him in honor of *yom tov."*

"Well, that's a nice gesture," said Reb Yankel. He turned towards the walls that were lined with *sefarim* all the way to the ceiling.

Pinney smiled to himself. Yes, it was a nice gesture, he agreed, and Ari deserved it. He was a good brother and a budding scholar.

"Pinney," asked Reb Yankel, "are you sure Ari won't buy the *sefer* for himself?"

"Oh, I know he won't," said Pinney. "I happen to know Ari is broke. You see, I was planning to borrow the money from him, but he told me that after certain expenses he has, he'll have no money left. And then we discussed the new *sefer*. We both kept admitting how much we'd love to buy it if we'd have the money."

Pinney frowned as he remembered what he gave up to get the money. He, too, was broke and had gone without spending money for the past few weeks. No soda! No snacks! No telephone calls to his friends!

"Here! Is this what you're looking for?" Reb Yankel handed him a thick large blue and green book with pictures of *gedolim* on the cover.

Pinney held the *sefer* tenderly: *The Lives of the Gedolim.* He looked at the pictures of Reb Moishe Feinstein, Reb Yaakov Kaminetzky, Rav Yitzchak Ruderman, the jewels of our generation. And in these five hundred pages were pearls of wisdom, life stories and episodes they were involved in as children, which already showed what promising *gedolim* they were going to be.

Pinney stroked the newly formed stubble on his chin. How he wanted this *sefer* for himself, to add to his growing collection of *sefarim* at home. But no, here was his chance to do a kindness for his brother.

"Ari is lucky to have such a generous brother like you," said Reb Yankel.

Pinney chuckled, "You know, Reb Yankel, when I think about all the fights we had as kids, I'm embarrassed. We fought over the silliest things, and boy, did we think it was important then!"

How foolish they had been, arguing and fighting over unimportant, trivial matters.

Pinney and Ari were a year apart in age and as different in their personalities as they were in their looks. Pinney was tall and broad with shiny, dark hair that curled in the humid summer air. His dark eyes gleamed with mischief and fun. He was quick and full of energy and could he seen late at night in the *beis midrash* swaying back and forth, frowning over a difficult passage in the *gemara*.

Ari, a year older, was fair and thin with large soft hazel eyes. He was easy going and had a gentle, sensitive nature. When he smiled, his face shone like the morning sunrise. He also could be seen late at night in the *beis midrash*, resting his face on his hands, leaning over his *gemara*.

"Should I wrap it up for you?" asked Reb Yankel.

"No, thanks," said Pinney. He held the precious *sefer* to his chest and paid the price of twenty dollars that he had worked for. He went to the door, peered out to make sure he wasn't being watched and quickly left the store.

The *sefarim* store was crowded when Ari entered. Reb Yankel had gone home and his partner, Reb Mendel, was there instead.

"Hello, Ari, can I help you?"

"Yes," said Ari in his quiet voice. "I'd like to buy the new *sefer* about the *gedolim*."

"It's just about sold out," said Reb Mendel. "Let me see if we have any left. Oh, here we are. You're in luck. One *sefer* left. Here it is!"

Ari looked at the picture of the *gedolim* on the cover. His eyes twinkled and his lips curled into a smile. "How Pinney is going to love this *sefer*," he thought. "How I would love it, too."

He was tempted to buy the *sefer* for himself. No one would be the wiser for it. But, no! He had decided a few weeks ago that he would like to buy Pinney a gift, in honor of *yom tov*. "I never bought Pinney anything," he realized, "and I know he wants this *sefer*. We discussed it so many times."

thought about how hard it had been to earn the money. He had been broke and had to find a few jobs between learning *sedarim* to get the extra cash.

Ari took the *sefer* and left the store.

He quickly returned to his room in the dormitory. Now, he thought, comes the hard part.

"I've got to get the *sefer* into Pinney's room when he's not there in order to surprise him. Hmmm . . ."

He thought a while. Suppertime! That should be a good time. Pinney would be in the dining room and then Ari could sneak into his room, and leave the *sefer* on Pinney's desk. Yes, that was a good plan!

Pinney ate his supper quickly. He had formed a plan. He would sneak into Ari's room now and leave the *sefer* on Ari's desk while Ari was eating his supper. He couldn't see Ari in the dining room but it was a large room and it was filled with hundreds of students.

Pinney *bentched* and got up quickly, the *sefer* hidden under his jacket. The dormitory halls were deserted. Pinney crept quietly into Ari's room, room 204, placed the *sefer* quickly on Ari's desk and ran through the halls back to his own room.

Ari walked quietly but quickly through the halls to room 301. Good! Pinney wasn't around. He placed the brand-new *sefer* on Pinney's desk and left the room as quietly as he had entered.

Pinney returned to his own room, smiling happily . . . and stopped in his tracks. The *sefer* was on his desk!!

"Now, how in the world, did I do that?" he wondered.

"I must have taken the wrong *sefer*." He shook his head and picked up the *sefer* from his desk. He hurried back to room 204, placed the *sefer* on Ari's desk and rushed back to his room.

Ari returned to his room happy to have the mission accomplished. He walked towards his bed and . . . stared. The *sefer*! It was still here. How . . .? He must have taken the wrong *sefer* to Pinney's room. He took the *sefer* and sighed. "Here we go again!" he thought as he walked quickly back to room 301.

Pinney slapped his forehead. "What in '*chalopchis*' is going on here?" he said aloud. His roommate, Shmuel, walked into the room.

"What's the matter, Pinney?" he asked.

"Look, Shmuel," Pinney said. "Look real good now. Do you see this *sefer*?"

"What's the matter with you, Pinney?" Shmuel asked, puzzled.

"I repeat," Pinney spoke in a louder voice. "I ask you to witness the evidence in my hands. Will the court please accept this evidence as exhibit number one! One brand new *sefer* on the life of the *gedolim*! Price twenty dollars! Five hundred pages! Do you or do you not see it in my hands?"

"Yes." Shmuel laughed. "I see it in your hands. But what's going on?"

"I'm not sure. Something funny's going on, but this *sefer* is going to it's destination — right now, if it's the last thing I do!"

He left the room and ran down the steps towards room 204.

Ari shook his head slowly from side to side and muttered under his breath. "Wha . . . how did . . . how can . . . what's . . . was . . ." How could the *sefer* be on his desk again? He couldn't understand it. Could he have taken the wrong *sefer* again to Pinney's room?

He looked at the *sefer* and studied it carefully: *The Life of the Gedolim.* He turned the *sefer* around in his hands over and over.

It was the right *sefer*. All right. Now, once and for all, he would take the right *sefer* to Pinney's room. He shook his head again in confusion as he began half walking — half running, to room 301.

Pinney ran! Ari ran! Faster and faster! With determination up the steps . . . down the steps. Closer to room 301. Closer to room 204. Around the corner. Around the turn. Closer . . . closer . . .

BANG! WHAM! The two brothers crashed into each other and fell, stumbling backwards onto the floor.

"Why don't you watch . . .?"

"What's the matter . . .?"

Pinney looked up. Ari looked up. The brothers stared into each other's faces. They were both holding their *sefer* on the *gedolim* in their hands.

Pinney looked at Ari's *sefer*. Ari looked at Pinney's *sefer*.

And then they started to laugh . . . and laugh . . . and laugh . . . and laugh.

Pinney laughed so hard he couldn't stop. Tears rolled down Ari's cheeks from his fit of laughter.

A crowd formed around the boys. "What's going on here?" asked a student as he, too, started to laugh.

"What's going on here?" asked another boy as he caught the infectious laughter. More and more boys gathered around the brothers who were hysterical with laughter; though no one else knew what was so funny.

Finally, Pinney pointed to Ari's *sefer* and stammered, "The . . . *sefer* . . . it's . . ." But another fit of laughter caught him and he couldn't continue.

Ari tried to speak. He pointed to the *sefer* in Pinney's hand and

started to laugh again.

Finally, Ari and Pinney stood up, each one handing to the other his own *sefer,* and walked away from the group of laughing boys.

The *bachurim* stared after them. One of them shook his head and exclaimed, "That must be a very funny *sefer.* Maybe I should buy it, too!"

The Clock

he clock! It had always been there as long as I could remember. It stood in the front hall looming over me. Its dull, cracked face, chiming out the time — 3:00 — 4:00 — 5:00. Sometimes it was right. Sometimes it wasn't.

"Why do you keep it?" asked my friend, Chasi. We stood in the hall, looking up at the huge wooden figure.

"It belonged to my father's father." I answered her. "Avrum Meir, my brother, is named after him. My grandfather shipped it out of Germany before the war."

That's really all I knew about its history. Chasi continued staring.

"But why?" Chasi asked. "Why would your grandfather send an old clock to America when I am sure he must have had more valuable possessions he would rather have saved!"

"I don't know!" I repeated.

"Maybe it's a mystery," Chasi said, her eyes shining.

"A mystery?"

"Yeah! Like maybe the clock is really an antique and worth millions."

"Oh, Chasi! That's silly!" I laughed. "Anyone can see it's not worth much. It's just an old broken clock."

"Then why did he smuggle it out?"

"He didn't smuggle it out! He shipped it out to my uncle in Canada and now we have it! There's no mystery to that."

"I still say there's something mysterious about the whole thing."

"Chasi, you're just searching for adventure. C'mon, we've got work to do."

I headed for the living room where Chasi and I were practicing our music lesson. We both had the same music teacher. Chasi had piano lessons. My family couldn't afford a piano, so I took lessons on the small keyboard. It was fun, but hard work.

"C'mon, Chasi! You start first, then I'll accompany you!"

She was good at it. I needed lots of practice.

"I wish I could play as well as you!"

"Well, Shani, you know I've been taking lessons for years. You just started. Be patient!"

"I can't be patient," I insisted. "I only have two weeks left till the *chasunah*."

"Shani, your brother can get married without you playing *'Od Yishama.'*"

"You don't understand, Chasi. You're the oldest in your family, but I'm the baby."

"What does that have to do with anything?" she asked.

I crawled to the middle of my bed and chewed on my pencil. "Avrum Meir is my only brother. All my sisters are married and I'm the baby of the family."

"So?"

"So, all my sisters are giving Avrum Meir presents. What can I give him? Avrum Meir is so special! He's my favorite brother! Well . . . you know what I mean. I heard my father say, he's one of the best boys in the *yeshivah*. He's going to be a real *talmid chacham* someday and he is so good and kind, I just have to give him something special."

"Why don't you just write him a poem or something?"

"I tried that. I even made a little book of pictures. I'm sure he doesn't expect anything from me. When I asked him what present he wanted he said, 'Shani, you stretch your smile two miles long and that'll be great!' He's funny! But then a few nights ago, when I was lying in bed, I got a great idea. We're making *sheva berachos* for him in our home. All my aunts and uncles and cousins will be there. When everyone is singing, I'm going to play 'Od Yishama' on the keyboard. Boy, will he be surprised! He doesn't even know I'm taking lessons."

"I still think he'd appreciate a poem more!"

"Anybody can write a poem!"

"Anybody can play the keyboard," Chasi answered. "Listen Shani, what I mean is, your brother Avrum Meir is so studious and loves to learn. I think he'd appreciate something more like a *sefer*."

"I thought about that! But I have no money to buy anything, and I don't know what kind of *sefer* to buy. So let's stop wasting time and practice!"

We played for an hour. Chasi played beautifully and I clumped those keys with ten left thumbs.

"I give up!" I said. "I'll never learn to play."

"Keep trying, Shani! You sounded better today than you did yesterday." She stood up. "I gotta go now! See you tomorrow."

That night at supper I forgot about my keyboard as I listened to Avrum Meir discuss his plans with my parents.

"We've got an apartment and Shulamis found a teaching job nearby so she won't have to travel."

"That's wonderful news!" my mother said. I knew my brother wanted to learn in the *yeshivah kollel* as long as he could. So I knew this was good news.

"Is the apartment close to us, too?" I asked.

Avrum Meir turned to me and laughed. "Close enough for you to visit anytime you want, Shanirany."

That was his pet name for me.

"I won't be a pest!" I promised.

"By the way," Avrum Meir said, "when am I going to see this surprise you have in store for me?"

At that moment I wanted to impress Avrum Meir more than anything else.

"You just wait and see," I said. "Nobody knows about this yet. It's going to be so big and special. It's going to be the best gift you ever got in your whole life."

Now, why did I say that?

"Hey, wow! Now you've really got me curious! What's up your sleeve, Shani?"

But I had said enough. I left the table feeling ashamed.

I called Chasi from my parents' bedroom and told her what I had said.

"Why did you do that?" She sounded annoyed.

"Chasi, I didn't call you to hear *mussar*. I need your help! You've got to help me come up with something big!"

"Avrum Meir really expects something special now and you've really got yourself in a fix, Shani."

"Some friend you are!"

"Okay! Okay! I'll think about it and I'll be over tomorrow. Okay?"

"Thanks!" I hung up.

The next two weeks were busy ones in my house, getting ready for the wedding. I still practiced 'Od Yishama' on my keyboard, but I couldn't get myself excited about it anymore.

"Shani, you're making too much of this," Chasi told me.

"No, I'm not," I said. "I know Avrum Meir will forgive me and anything I give him will be fine. But you don't understand, Chasi. I want to give him something big, something that he'll remember all his life!"

"How about life insurance?"

"Ha! Ha! Very funny!"

Maybe I was making too big a thing out of this. Avrum Meir probably didn't expect anything big from me. Playing 'Od Yishama' on the keyboard was no big deal, but at least it showed him I cared and wanted to do something nice for him.

I plunked those keys and kept to the beat as I hummed the words.

"Hey, Shani! You're getting to be not bad," Chasi told me the night before the wedding.

The clock in the hall chimed. 10:00 . . .11:00 . . .12:00. It was now only 6:00. The gong gonged wrong again. Chasi and I went to the hall and stared at the old clock that stood eight feet tall and chimed the wrong time.

It seemed to have a personality of its own. We both stood staring as the hands of the clock moved steadily toward the hour . . . the wrong hour.

"Do you think . . .?" Chasi began.

"Do I think what?" I asked.

"Well, maybe your Zaidy wasn't really interested in the clock. Maybe there was something else valuable he wanted to get out of the country."

"You mean, maybe he hid jewelry or money in the clock?"

Chasi shrugged. We both put our hands over the clock, feeling the rough wooden exterior. On the back towards the bottom, we felt a rusty wooden latch. We tried pulling on it, but nothing happened. We banged, we pushed, we knocked. The latch was bent and stuck.

Feverish excitement filled me. I felt my heart slamming against my ribs.

I ran to get some tools from my father's kit. We banged again. Suddenly the hinge broke and a small paneled door as big as my hand slid open, revealing a secret compartment. Our hearts beat faster than a speeding fire engine.

"There's something in there," Chasi whispered, in a voice that sounded like a scream.

I reached in and pulled out a soft faded velvet bag. Was it full of diamonds, rubies, pearls? My knees were shaking and I could hardly stand. I swallowed a few times and finally croaked, "It's the treasure my Zaidy wanted to get out of the country."

We didn't open the bag. I ran to show it to my parents. Chasi followed me. My father was as excited as I was.

"I always thought there was something mysterious about the clock, but I could never find a secret compartment."

"It's very small. My hand could hardly fit in it," I said.

My father slowly opened the blue velvet bag as we all watched breathlessly. I anticipated seeing a brilliant array of colored jewels as he removed . . . a few old crumpled papers!

"Papers!" I almost choked. "Is that it?"

I was so disappointed. Here I thought there might be a real treasure and all there was was some old papers. But then I looked at my father. His eyes were enormous and he had an expression on his face that I had never seen before.

"My . . . my father's *chidushei Torah,*" he said in a voice filled with awe.

"What is that, Abba?" I asked, as I realized there was something here that was more than I understood.

My mother brought my father a chair and he sat down. He placed his hand on his forehead and spoke softly.

"My father was a great *talmid chacham*. He knew all of *Shas*. I always knew he wrote *chidushim* on the Torah. These are his explanations and thoughts on the Torah he learned. But I never knew what happened to them. We all thought they were destroyed during the war. But here they are."

"That's what he was smuggling out of Germany!" I trembled from the excitement that welled up inside of me. "He knew he couldn't send out his works of Torah, so he hid them in his clock and had the clock shipped to Canada."

"Wow!" Chasi shouted! "You can see that that was more valuable and important to him than anything else."

My father held the papers tenderly as tears filled his eyes. "What a treasure this is," he said. "What a gold mine of Torah wisdom. Thank you, my little Shanele, for finding it for me."

I suddenly knew what I wanted desperately. I whispered my plan into his ear. He smiled and kissed me.

"I agree," he said. "It will fit the picture perfectly."

"What picture?" Chasi asked. "Who's talking about pictures?"

Four days later at Avrum Meir's *sheva berachos*, I made a little speech. "My brother, Avrum Meir, is named after my Zaidy who was a great *talmid chacham.*"

Avrum Meir looked at me with a twinkle in his eyes. He knew this was the moment that I was waiting for, to present him with my big surprise.

"Avrum Meir, I don't know how to make fancy speeches. I'm only your kid sister, but I do know you deserve this."

I handed him the faded manuscript, now bound carefully in a leather cover.

Avrum Meir had a puzzled expression on his face. He stared at the manuscript for so long, till his *kallah* finally snapped him out of it when she asked, "Avrum Meir, what is it?"

"It's my Zaidy's *divrei Torah*," he said. "I've often heard about them, but we thought they were destroyed during the war." His voice shook. "Where did you get this?"

I told him and the rest of the family the whole story. Everyone was talking at the same time.

I never did get to play 'Od Yishama' on the keyboard but I had a greater thrill watching Avrum Meir. The effect on him was as if I had handed him the most precious gift in the world. And maybe I did!

A Heart in the Hand

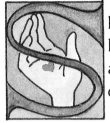S he was going to eat alone again. All the other girls had gathered around their favorite tables, laughing and talking. Chaya walked silently to her seat in the corner.

"Tuna fish again!" she thought.

She tried to keep her mind off the morning's events. It really wasn't much different than any day. The hall was filled with the usual morning crowd, but no one paid attention to her. Chaya could hear bits and pieces of conversations, but none were addressed to her.

"Hi, Ariella! I love your sweater!"

"Did you do your science project yet? Come over after school and we'll work on it together."

"Don't forget the Chanukah party at my house."

Chaya could hear the sounds coming from far away as if from a whirling wind.

"Henni, I love your necklace!"

"Thanks."

Chaya turned around. Henni was wearing a small beaded necklace. In the center was a golden heart.

"I strung the beads myself," said Henni, "and my mother bought me the heart."

Chaya thought it was the prettiest necklace she had ever seen.

"I like it, too," she said softly.

Henni didn't answer and turned away. "Maybe she didn't hear me," Chaya thought.

During class, Chaya volunteered for most of the jobs nobody wanted. Nobody seemed to notice or care.

In the middle of English, Ora passed a note to Chaya. Chaya was excited. No one had ever passed her a note before. She quickly opened the crinkled paper.

"Don't forget the Chanukah party at my house. You're all invited."

Chaya smiled and turned around to face Ora. As she did, her smile evaporated. Ora had a frown on her face and was pointing frantically to Henni. The note was for Henni, not for her! Her cheeks flaming, Chaya passed the note down to Henni.

Later at recess she asked Ora. "Am I invited, too?"

Ora looked at her with distaste. When she spoke, her voice was like an icicle. "The note wasn't for you."

Chaya felt a terrible loneliness digging into her bones, and now she was still alone, eating her lunch.

Chaya saw her reflection in the mirror behind her. Pale blue eyes stared back at her from a thin freckled face. Chaya pushed her stringy black hair out of her eyes and willed herself not to care.

But she did care. She cared very much. So she wasn't pretty, or smart, or rich. So she had bony knees that had scabs on them. She still had feelings!

Didn't the girls know how much it hurt being an outsider? Didn't they see how much it hurt being ignored and forgotten? Chaya's lunch turned to rocks in her stomach and her throat felt as if there was a tight band around it and she couldn't swallow. In the afternoon, Chaya threw herself into her work to drown out her pain.

"If they ignore me, I'll just ignore them!" she thought.

Mrs. Steinberg was explaining the homework assignment. "Each girl should write one or two paragraphs on any familiar topic. Something everybody knows about, but you must write from an original point of view."

Sora Nechama raised her hand. "Can we make it up?"

"No! It should be something real and familiar to you, like a picnic in the park or a trip to the zoo. The main thing is to be descriptive."

Henni was enthusiastic. "Last winter, I got lost in a snowstorm! Can I write about that?"

"Yes, but remember, the main thing is to try to be descriptive. Describe a party, the people, the food, your feelings."

Chaya wondered what she could write about. On her way home from school, she stopped at the creek. She sat on a rock and stared at the raging water.

The creek was Chaya's favorite place. She came to it often to think and relax. The ground was damp and the wind was chilly and raw in the thin sunshine.

"Maybe, I'll write about the creek," she thought.

The water swirled and rushed down the slope, crashing against the stones and churning up little whirlpools of foam. Chaya opened her notebook and began to write.

The creek bubbled swiftly on the stones . . .!

Chaya looked up and stared at the water. Why didn't the girls like her? Why weren't they nice to her? She hadn't done anything to them! What makes one girl popular and another not?

Hashem made us all, she thought.

Isn't it a *mitzvah* to make people feel good? Doesn't the Torah command us to be kind? How could you love someone if you always ignore him or her?

Chaya felt the breeze on her hot cheeks. She felt so alone, as if there wasn't another person in the world besides her. She felt as if she would sit there by the creek the rest of her life and stare at the stones and water.

Suddenly, salty rivers were running down her cheeks. Once the tears started they flowed swift and easy.

Chaya felt lonely and confused. She began to write quickly and furiously. Pen and tears flowed together as shadows deepened and daylight drained away. One cloud hung above catching the last sunlight in a blaze of rose pink. Chaya put her notebook in her book bag and ran home.

The next day, Chaya was the first one in her seat.

"Hi, Henni! Hi, Ariella! Hi, Ora!" Would anyone say hello to her? Chaya wondered. She looked up and saw Henni in the middle of a circle of girls, laughing happily. She was wearing her heart necklace again. Chaya couldn't help staring at it.

"But I won't tell her again that I like it," she thought stubbornly.

Mrs. Steinberg called on Sora Nechama to read her homework assignment. It was a good report. It told how miserable she was when she had had the chicken pox.

Ora was next. She told about her trip to Canada and how scary it was to fly in a plane.

Mrs. Steinberg looked around the room, "Chaya, please read yours next."

Chaya walked up to the front of the class. Her knees were wobbly and her voice came out timid and shaky.

> There are different kinds of pain. They all hurt. When you fall on the cement and scrape your knee, that hurts. When you touch a hot pot and burn your finger, that hurts. When you get a splinter in your thumb, that hurts.
>
> There are other kinds of hurt. When you have no friends, that hurts too. When kids make fun of you and don't invite you to their house, that hurts. When they laugh at you or ignore you and don't want to be your friend, that hurts.
>
> I think the hurt that hurts the most is being left out and lonely.

Chaya spoke in a low voice, just above a whisper, but the class remained so quiet, every word was audible.

Chaya kept her head down. She didn't want to see if anyone was looking at her.

"That was a very good report," Mrs. Steinberg said. "Very descriptive." The teacher's praise fell on Chaya like water on parched grass.

"May I please leave the room?" she asked. She needed to be

alone. She couldn't bear to face the class and hear comments on her report. Would they make fun of it?

After a few minutes, she returned to her room. All eyes turned to her, but Mrs. Steinberg continued teaching.

Chaya sat down in her seat. What was this? A small package wrapped in a brown paper lunch bag was on her desk. Was this some kind of joke? She was about to throw the bag away when she saw the words "to Chaya" written on it.

Chaya was puzzled. She put her hand in the bag and stared open mouthed at the contents. It was the little heart necklace. There was a card next to it.

"I'm sorry! Can we be friends?
                    Henni"

Chaya held the necklace tightly in her fist and looked up. There was a lump in her throat. She saw Henni smiling at her. Chaya smiled back and nodded slowly, still holding the necklace tightly.

She held it during History and Math, till the recess bell rang.

"Want to play jump rope?" Ariella asked.

"I don't know how to jump rope," she said.

"I'll teach you," Henni laughed, and put her arm around her.

"Thank you for the necklace, Henni," Chaya said. "But I really can't take it from you. It's too pretty and besides, it must be expensive."

"That's all right."

"No! I really can't." She opened her hand and gave Henni back her necklace.

"Look!" Henni pointed excitedly. "You have a heart in your hand!"

"What?" Chaya looked at her hand. In the center where she had been pressing the golden heart tightly, was embedded in her skin a tiny heart shape.

Henni laughed, "Now we're true friends from the heart."

Cartons and Cars

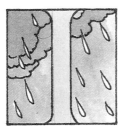f I don't get a move on, I'm going to be late for *Shabbos.*" Yankie rushed out of the store with his shopping bag. It was starting to drizzle.

"Hey, Yankie," called Berel. "Are you going back to *yeshivah* now?"

"Sure am," answered Yankie. "Need a ride? But hurry, I'm late, I still have to stop at the shoemaker and barber."

"Okay," said Berel, putting his packages into Yankie's car.

"How's it going, Berel?" Yankie asked, as he drove the car down the narrow Scranton Road.

"Baruch Hashem; I'm finally starting to understand the *shiur.* It was real hard at first but I kept working and working at it."

"Only way to go." Yankie smiled. He remembered his first year in *yeshivah.* It seemed such a long time ago. Now he was in *Beis Midrash* and *Baruch Hashem,* the learning was going good.

"Oh, by the way," said Berel. "I hear you get a *mazel tov.*"

"That's right. Thank you. I got engaged last week." That reminded him. He also wanted to call his *kallah* before *Shabbos* to wish her a good *Shabbos.*

"Will you still be here after you get married?" asked Berel.

"I hope to be learning in the *kollel* here, *im yirtzeh Hashem.* So we'll be here for a while."

"Hey, isn't that Reb Shmuel waving to us to stop?"

"Yes, I think so," said Yankie. "Maybe he needs a ride too — Reb Shmuel, need a ride?"

"No, thank you, Yankie," said Reb Shmuel, "but I need a

favor. I was supposed to deliver these cartons of cheese to the *yeshivah* before *Shabbos*, but my truck broke down. Could you possibly do it for me?"

Yankie was worried. He still had so much to do before *Shabbos*. If he delivered the cheese, he might not have time to stop at the barber to get a haircut before *Shabbos*. He also needed to stop at the cleaners, he just remembered. But a *mitzvah* is a *mitzvah*, he told himself.

"Sure, Reb Shmuel, we'll do it."

Reb Shmuel smiled gratefully.

"But aren't you in a hurry?" asked Berel, getting out of the car.

"I am, Berel, but you can't pass up a *mitzvah* if it comes your way."

Berel was impressed. It was his first year in *yeshivah* and he was learning new things every day. *Gemara, Mishnayos, Chumash, Halachah* . . . and these *bachurim* were living the Torah they were learning.

"I'll help you load the car," he said.

It took the two boys a long time to carry the heavy cartons of cheese and put them into the car.

"Let's stuff them in the back here," said Yankie, breathing hard. The cartons were heavy and they took up most of the space in the small old car.

"I feel like I'm in a cocoon," said Berel, as they resumed their drive.

It was dark and crowded in the car and he was uncomfortable. The clear sky had deepened to a dark gray. The rain was coming down hard. Yankie had to drive slowly. He was aware of the darkness closing in around them. The road was slippery and the windshield wipers were swinging back and forth, back and forth.

A fork of lighting licked down through the sky. Thunder rolled ominously.

"Yesterday," said Berel, "after night *seder* I saw . . ." Berel never finished the words. A horn blasted. Tires shrieked. Suddenly the car skidded and screeched to a lurching spin. Yankie held the wheel tightly, his fingers gripping it, trying to gain control of the spinning car. Icy panic held him in a freezing grip. The car began spinning and weaving down the road, heading straight for the incline. It made a final screech and bounced off the incline and rolled over and over till it hit the bottom of the ditch and lay face down in the grass. Yankie caught his breath and scrambled out of the car. He crawled to the other side and helped Berel out. The boys staggered to their feet.

"Berel are . . . are you all right?" Yankie asked him.

"I . . . think so," stammered Berel.

He was as shaken as Yankie was, but nothing hurt him. He couldn't believe it. The car was upside down, twisted and ruined. And there they were standing in front of it, not only alive but completely unhurt. Yankie stood with his mouth open, dazed and shocked.

In a short time the police came. One policeman was speaking to him. Yankie heard his voice coming to him through a fog.

"You boys sure are a lucky bunch."

"What happened, officer?" asked Yankie.

"I'm not sure, it seems your car skidded and rolled over this incline here." He scratched his head.

"Well, I'll be!" he muttered. "You guys must have something going for you. A miracle, that's what it is, a miracle." Again he stared at the car. "You guys were saved by those cheese boxes."

"What do you mean, officer?" asked Yankie shakily.

"Well, the way I see it is that the car roof should have caved in with all that pressure, but those boxes of cheese held up the roof of the car so it didn't cave in on you. That's what saved you, a bunch of cheese boxes. Yes, indeed!"

Cheese cartons! The cheese cartons they were supposed to bring to the *yeshivah*. Yankie looked at Berel and Berel looked at Yankie. They nodded.

Shiluchei mitzvah einon nizukin — When one is on his way to do a *mitzvah*, he has special protection, the *Gemara* teaches.

I wasn't there but I heard the story from Baruch, who heard it from Moshe, who heard it from Dovid, who heard it from Berel. And now you heard it from me.

The King's Delight

isroel Meir sat in The King's Delight dairy restaurant with his head lowered.

What a day! What a day! He had been trying to find a job now for the past few weeks and he was almost ready to give up.

"But how could I give up?" he thought.

His wife, Deena, had encouraged him. "Don't worry, Yisroel Meir, *Hashem* will help. I'm sure something will turn up soon."

"But when? When?" thought Yisroel Meir dejectedly. His newborn baby, Chana Malka, needed him. His lips curled into a hint of a smile as he thought of her innocent big eyes and toothless grin.

A feeling of tenderness and protectiveness came over him. But what was he going to do?

Right now he was tired and, oh, so hungry. He hadn't eaten since breakfast and even then only a quick coffee and two cookies.

Yisroel Meir sniffed the aroma coming from the kitchen in the back. Tantalizing sweet smells of cinnamon, cheese cake and sweet and sour dishes filled the restaurant. His mouth watered and his heart ached.

"What will you have?" the waiter asked.

Yisroel Meir looked at the menu. $3.50 . . . $5.00 . . . $7.00. He placed his hand in his pocket and pulled out some change.

How he would have loved to have a knish and some hot soup. But he barely had enough money for the bus fare home.

"Uh . . . I'll have . . . a cup of coffee and a few crackers, please!"

His head was throbbing and he was so very hungry. But, worst of all was his feeling of rejection.

Over and over, he had gone from one place to another to find a job, and over and over he kept hearing, "Come back when you have experience." How could he get experience if nobody was willing to give him a job to get experience?

He had tried the toy shop, the bakery, the new paper factory and dozens of other places. What else could he do?

He was so hungry and tired. He felt like putting his head down on his arms and having a good cry.

Yisroel Meir thought of the one option he had left open to him and he shuddered at the prospect.

"You're welcome to come into the business any time," his Uncle Harry had offered him.

But Uncle Harry lived in Miles City, Montana. That would mean moving away from the big city with all its advantages of a good Jewish education for his little Chana Malka. There were hardly any Jews living in Miles City, Montana, and certainly no good Jewish schools. It was no place to raise a Jewish family. How could he do that to his wife and children?

"But if I have no choice," Yisroel Meir thought, "then I'm going to take that offer. I just can't keep going on like this." He was ready to give up.

Right now, all he really wanted was a good, hearty meal. It wouldn't solve his problem, he knew, but it sure would lift his spirits.

Reb Zalman Finkelman walked into The King's Delight restaurant. He sat at a table near the corner and looked at the menu.

Boy, was he hungry! "I'll take a vegetable soup, cheese blintzes, a potato knish, salad and a piece of fudge cake with a cup of coffee." The waiter wrote down his order and left.

Reb Zalman looked around the brightly lit room. The restaurant was not crowded this time of day, he thought.

His eyes set upon Yisroel Meir. "My! But that poor guy looks unhappy," he thought. "In fact, he looks like he can use a good meal."

Just then the waiter approached Yisroel Meir and set down his cup of coffee and a few crackers.

Reb Zalman stared horrified. "That's all he's going to eat? He looks like he's ready to fall over from hunger and fatigue, and all he's having are some crackers and coffee?"

Yisroel Meir drank his coffee slowly, his mood becoming more and more discouraged and sad.

The waiter returned with Reb Zalman's order. "Here your are, sir."

"Thank you." Reb Zalman got up to wash. He looked at his tray. Then he looked back at the young man. He shook his head sadly.

Suddenly, he picked up his tray and carried it over to Yisroel Meir.

"Excuse me," he said. Yisroel Meir looked up. Reb Zalman was surprised. "Why, he's so young. He's hardly more than a boy," he thought.

"Yes?" Yisroel Meir asked.

Reb Zalman cleared his throat. "Ahem! I was wondering if you could please do me a favor?"

"I'll try," said Yisroel Meir.

"You see, I'm in a big hurry and I just ordered this big meal, and

I find I just don't have the time to eat it. I hate to see good food go to waste. Could you please help me out? I really would appreciate it."

Yisroel Meir was astonished. "You mean, you want me to eat your dinner?"

"Please! You'd be doing me a great favor."

"But . . . I . . . I have no money to pay you."

"Oh, no, don't worry about it. I have no time anyway. Just take it, please." He didn't give Yisroel Meir a chance to think it out. He started moving away.

Yisroel Meir could barely get the words out, "Thank you."

"Thank *you*," Reb Zalman said and quickly rushed out of the restaurant.

Yisroel Meir couldn't believe his good luck. He looked at his scrumptious meal and got up to wash.

"What a *baal chesed*," he thought. "And he doesn't even know me."

Yisroel Meir ate slowly and felt relaxed. When he finished, his headache was gone and his stomach was full.

"*Reb Yid*," he said softly under his breath, "you have no idea what you've done for me. You are truly 'The King's Delight.'" He smiled at his own words.

"Maybe I'll just try one more place." He felt his strength returning and became eager and encouraged. "There's a *sefarim* store at the corner of Westbrook and Key. Maybe they can use some help." He left the store feeling lighthearted and full of hope again.

The owner of the *sefarim* store was overworked. He was thrilled with Yisroel Meir's offer.

Yisroel Meir got the job, and because he was a hard, ambitious worker, he worked his way up, and he eventually became the manager of the store.

And Reb Zalman Finkelman never did find out how his one small act of *chesed* changed a whole family's life forever.

A Story

rs. Mintz told us to write a story for homework tomorrow. All I wrote so far was my name in the left-hand corner — Raizel Rohr. Well, it's late and my pencil is chewed up, and I better get started . . . so here goes!

THE PRINCESS AND THE GIFT OF DAY

Once upon a time in a land far away at the end of the earth there stood a tall majestic palace among huge mountains covered with crystal snow. Its walls were built of solid gold and its floors were lined with silver.

Inside the palace lived a king so wise and great that everyone in the kingdom loved and respected and admired him.

"We are so lucky to have a king as great as our king," people would often say.

Everyone in the kingdom took their troubles to the king. When something went wrong the king solved the problem with truth and justice.

The courtyards were filled daily with those whose needs were met. The king never turned anyone away. No person was ever left empty-handed or disappointed. The king showered gifts of food, clothing and gold to all who came. All one had to do was ask and it was his.

The country was rich with fields of golden harvest, orange groves, and delicacies so sweet and pure. The people lived in a state of pure joy.

People in other countries never heard of the great king and his being was a mystery to them. They lived far away and news of the generous and mighty king never reached their ears.

The king had one daughter, the princess, whom he loved dearly. She was more precious to him than all his riches. The princess loved her father immensely as did everyone who knew him.

One day, the king called his daughter to his private chambers. The princess dressed in a garment of woven white silk and entered her father's chamber.

"My dear princess," the king said fondly. "You are very special to me and I want to give you a gift that will make you happy. Ask for anything you desire and your wish is my command."

The princess spoke softly. "My father, I am happy now. I have everything I could possibly want or need. I live in this beautiful palace surrounded by riches and pleasures of all kinds. What more could I possibly desire?"

The king was still not satisfied. "I will give you a gift. I will give you something very unique."

The princess waited to hear. The king thundered, "I will give you the gift of . . . DAY!"

The princess opened her eyes in surprise. "Day?" she repeated. She didn't understand. What kind of gift was this? "But Father," the princess asked, "what shall I do with this gift of day?"

The king smiled benevolently. "That is up to you, my dear child. You may do whatever you see fit with your 'day'. But that is my gift to you. One full 'day', to do with as your heart desires."

The princess left the palace in confusion. She took a walk in the beautiful palace gardens.

Her father, the king, had given her the gift of day. "But what shall I do with this gift?"

She sat on a smooth rock and thought deeply. "My father is so good, so considerate, always looking out for the benefit of others — and now he has given me this gift. And I don't know what to do with it!"

A bird nearby sang a sweet song and the princess gazed at it. "How I wish I could give my father a gift, too. But what can I give him? He is the ruler over everything. He does not need my gifts." Her father was so strong and noble, but only the people of her country knew about him.

As the sun shone brightly on her face, the princess suddenly stood up and exclaimed, "I know! That is what I will do with my gift. I will travel to countries far and wide and tell all the world how great my father is. In that way, I can repay him a little bit for what he has done for me."

The princess set out immediately. Time was short and precious. Her gift was one day and no more. The day would pass quickly.

The princess climbed into her ivory vessel which flew faster than the wind and began her journey.

She traveled through mountains and deserts, through grassy slopes where wild flowers swayed in the breeze, through forests and rivers, through treacherous storms and blinding blizzards.

Sharp winds whipped the sea into furious waves but the princess went on. Threatening shapes appeared and disappeared, but the princess pushed on. She had a gift, a purpose, and her gallant effort spurred her on.

Wherever she went, the princess told the people about her father's might, his wisdom, how he sat on his throne of mercy and governed with truth and justice, with compassion and kindness.

How he ruled his county with love and understanding. How powerful he was and protected his subjects from harm. How he opened his treasures to his people and granted each person's request as a father to a child.

With each country that she traveled through, the people understood the greatness of her father, the king.

The wind blew through the trees whispering, "Hurry, hurry, princess, the day will soon be over. The palace gates will soon be closing. Night is approaching."

The princess rode faster. One more ocean to cross and the sun would soon set. Her gift of day would soon be over. There was no time to waste.

Suddenly, out of the waters rose a creature with eyes like fire and clamped its jaws about the ship's brow. Soon, more and more creatures leaped up out of the waves, trying to destroy the ship with their ferocious jaws. The princess fought the creatures one by one.

"I will not let them destroy my ship," she repeated over and over again as she hit each creature with her golden rod. "I must return to my father. Nothing will stop me."

One by one, the wild creatures swam away in fright and the princess sailed on.

As the last rays of the orange-red sun began to set behind the vast mountains, the princess entered the palace gates, tired but contented. She had accomplished what she had set out to do.

As night fell, the king beckoned her to his chamber.

There was silence in the golden halls of the palace as the princess entered.

The king rose to greet his daughter. He had missed his only child. "My daughter, it is good to see you. Tell me, what have you done with your gift?"

The princess bowed. "My father," she cried. And as she spoke, her tears fell to the floor and turned to diamonds. "You are so good to me and my heart is full of love for you. I used your gift, the day, to travel far and wide and tell the whole world about your greatness, about the wondrous good you do, about how lucky we are to have a king like you."

The king approached the princess. "My daughter, you please me very much. You are not only beautiful but wise as well."

He kissed his daughter on her head and the princess realized that making her father happy was the best gift she herself could have received for now she felt closer to her father than ever before.

The story is a *mashal*. The king is *Hashem,* and we the Jewish people are the princess. The gift of day is the gift of life. *Hashem* has given us this precious gift to see what we can do with it.

It is up to us to use this gift wisely. The best way we can repay

Hashem for all He has done for us is to show the world how great He is, to fill our lives with *mitzvos* and good deeds, learn *Hashem's* Torah which will make our lives rich with purpose and meaning and bring us closer to *Hashem,* our Father, our King.

I hope Mrs. Mintz likes my story. Maybe she'll like it so much, she'll publish it in a book someday.

Drought

t hadn't rained for nine months in *Eretz Yisrael*. Dov Dov watched the men swaying back and forth. There were *minyanim* reciting *Tehillim* around the clock. When one *minyan* ended, another one started. A special prayer beginning **Aneinu Borei Olam . . .** had been added to the blessing *Shema Koleinu* in *Shemoneh Esrei*.

Some people fasted, some cried, and all prayed with one common purpose — rain!

Dov Dov was visiting in *Eretz Yisrael*, with his cousins, the Kaufmans. It was quite an experience for him.

At 6:00 each morning the radio woke everyone up with its broadcast of *"Mah Tovu."* Uncle Aryeh told Dov Dov that in the European *shtetl*, the *shammas* of the *shul* would make his rounds each morning, knocking on doors, waking people for *Shacharis* with the call, "Jews, Jews, holy and pure, wake up to serve your Creator."

On the way home from *shul*, Dov Dov asked Uncle Aryeh about the rain situation. "I know rain is important and all that, but after all, it's only rain. It's not something really important, like sickness or war! It's just something natural. The weatherman knows whether it's going to rain or not."

Uncle Aryeh walked slowly and answered him, "Rain is not just a natural event, Dov Dov. It's not just a coincidence. When *Hashem* created the world, He made it in such a way that all physical things would be dependent on Him. Rain in its proper time is a sign of blessing from *Hashem* and the relationship between us and *Hashem* depends on our actions."

"I know you depend on the rain for your crops," Dov Dov said, "but I still don't understand what rain has to do with *Hashem*."

Uncle Aryeh stopped and looked at Dov Dov kindly. "Dov Dov, rain is the truest measure of showing *Hashem's* connection to the world. Having rain shows that we're worthy of having a special relationship with Him."

He stopped for a minute, looked up toward the sky, then added, "Not having rain is the most powerful call to *teshuvah*."

Dov Dov was impressed. "How do we do *teshuvah*?"

"Well, first of all," said Uncle Aryeh, "it's a *mitzvah* to call out to *Hashem* in hard times. Calling out in prayer is one of the ways of doing *teshuvah*. When we call out to *Hashem*, we show that we realize that everything comes from Him."

At breakfast time, they continued the conversation. Between mouthfuls of home-baked fresh bread, *leben*, cucumbers and tomatoes, Dov Dov said, "In America, we don't worry about things like rain."

"That's because you take it for granted," said Eitan, Dov Dov's cousin.

"We depend on our rain for our crops and our livelihood," said Rivka, who was two years older than Dov Dov. "The Kineret is now at its lowest level."

"But it's even more than that," said Aunt Esther. "When we *daven* for rain it's not just a request for rain, but a request that we be returned to a closer relationship to *Hashem*, to the relationship of love between *Hashem* and us which existed when we accepted the Torah at *Har Sinai*."

In America, when Dov Dov woke up on a cloudy day with rain

dripping down his window, he complained, "Ugh! Another dreary day! Nothing to do!" Life was very different in *Eretz Yisrael*.

"C'mon," six-year-old Efraim called. "Let's go on our trip already!"

Aunt Esther was hanging up the laundry on the *mirpeset*, the balcony. Rivka was washing the floor. She poured a bucket of soapy water on the stone floor. Then she used a *sponga*, a kind of big windshield wiper — and swooshed the water out to the *mirpeset* and on to the street below. "I'll be ready soon," she said.

Dov Dov went out to the *chatzeir* to wait. It was like a big backyard where a lot of buildings joined together.

Dov Dov thought of all the places he had seen.

He had been to Yericho, one of the oldest cities in the world. They had gone by truck and brought back *s'chach* to cover the *succah*.

He had been to Tzefas, high in the Upper Galil mountains. The cool air and breath-taking view were great. He saw the famous *shul* of the Arizal who lived there in the sixteenth century when the city's rabbi was Rav Yosef Caro who wrote the *Shulchan Aruch*.

He had seen the secret tunnel of King Chizkiyahu, which he had dug in order to escape from King Sancherev of Ashur.

And, of course, he had been to the *Kotel*, the only wall left of the *Beis Hamikdash*. The first time Dov Dov saw it, he just stared and stared. "Just imagine! Two thousand years ago, our *Beis Hamikdash* stood here and the *Kohanim* brought *korbanos* every day. For two thousand years, Jews have come from all over the world to *daven* and pour out their hearts here."

Today the family was going to *Kever Rachel*. Dov Dov stared up at the cloudless, blue sky. Still, no rain.

"We're ready," Eitan called.

They started out from Yerushalayim and had a short ride of fifteen minutes through hilly land to Beis Lechem, where *Rachel Imeinu* is buried.

Dov Dov could see olive groves and vineyards and Arabs riding their donkeys.

Inside the dome, Aunt Esther began saying *Tehillim* and Dov Dov could see that she was crying. Uncle Aryeh was whispering and Dov Dov moved closer to him to hear what he was saying.

"Rachel *Imeinu*, you died on this very road when your son Binyamin was born. The *navi* Yirmiyahu said, 'A voice is heard in Heaven as you weep for your children and beg *Hashem* to have pity on His nation.' Please, Rachel *Imeinu*, plead to *Hashem*, beg Him to have mercy on His nation now, and ask for His keys to unlock the rain."

Dov Dov moved away from Uncle Aryeh and stood in a corner by himself. "I'm not very good at this, *Hashem*," he whispered. "I don't know exactly how to say what I mean, but I turn to You, *Hashem*, as a servant turns to his Master. You know my feelings. I want to be good, to make You proud of me. I can't promise I'll always be good, but I'll try to learn more Torah, *daven* more slowly, do more *chesed*, give more *tzedakah*. Please, please, Rachel, our mother, ask *Hashem* to send us rain!"

Dov Dov stood for a while, feeling a chill run through his body, till Uncle Aryeh gently tapped him on the shoulder. "Come, Dov Dov, we must go!"

On the bus ride home, Dov Dov kept looking out the window. Not a cloud in sight! He was disappointed. Somehow, he had felt that his prayers at *Kever Rachel* would bring rain.

Aunt Esther saw his disappointment. "Don't give up, Dov Dov.

A *yid* has to keep on going, never to give up. We never know when our help will come. Just keep on *davening*. Don't give up."

When they got home Aunt Esther and Rivka went to get supper started. Uncle Aryeh and Eitan went shopping and Dov Dov went to sit on a stone in the *chatzeir*. He was lonely and upset.

Soon, Efraim joined him. He was holding a *Chumash* in his hands.

"I'm going to learn *Chumash*," he announced proudly. "I'm going to learn extra Torah so *Hashem* will send us rain." His trust in *Hashem* was simple and complete.

"*Bereishis*, in the beginning; *barah Elokim*, *Hashem* created; *es hashamayim*, the Heavens; *ve'es ha'aretz*, and the Earth."

As he chanted on, Dov Dov felt something tickle his nose. Then it tickled his forehead, then his cheeks. Soon, Efraim and Dov Dov lifted their faces upwards as they realized what was happening. RAIN!!

In their excitement they bumped into each other as they stood up to rush into the streets.

They met Uncle Aryeh, Eitan, Aunt Esther, Rivka and dozens of people running into the streets laughing and crying, "*Geshem! Geshem!*"

Old men, young boys, mothers holding their babies in their arms, children running in circles, and everywhere, everyone was shouting, "*Baruch Hashem! Baruch Hashem!*"

The rain was coming down hard now, and Dov Dov couldn't tell the difference between the raindrops and the tears pouring down people's cheeks.

He let the rain flow down his face into his mouth. A simple thing like rain and it meant so much. Dov Dov never knew such excitement and joy in all his life.

That night he told Uncle Aryeh, "I think it was because of Efraim's learning that the rains came."

Uncle Aryeh beamed at him. "It was *everybody's* combined efforts of *tefillah* and learning and desire to do *teshuvah* that reached *shamayim* and brought us the rain."

And Dov Dov felt that he had been a part of a miracle, an experience he would never forget.